The Wife 101 Workbook

The Wife 101 Workbook

A'ndrea J. Wilson

Divine
Garden
Press

Soperton, Georgia

Published by Divine Garden Press
www.divinegardenpress.com

ISBN-13: 978-0615593524
ISBN-10: 0615593526

Cover Photograph: © Zhelobkov/Dreamstime.com

Cover Design: A'ndrea J. Wilson

Table of Contents

Letter from the Author

Dear Reader/Wife 101 Student,

Wife 101 was a good idea that turned into a great book. As an author, I was overwhelmed by the initial responses from those who read the novel and wanted more. Who knew that a story about a misguided woman taking a course on womanhood could spark change in the lives of its readers?

The Wife 101 Workbook is a direct result of reader feedback. Many women reported writing in their books or pulling out paper and pens while reading the book because they too wanted to experience the Wife 101 course. I will admit that I fought with the idea because I wasn't too thrilled about putting out a complementary book three months after the release of the novel, but I knew it was the right thing to do.

What you hold in your hand now is an opportunity to reflect on the 31 lessons of the book, the 31 verses in Proverbs 31, and the 13 classes that make up Wife 101. If you have not already read the novel, I highly recommended either reading the novel prior to completing the workbook or simultaneous to completing the workbook. The lessons in the workbook follow along with the lessons in the novel and have mirroring titles for easy use. Use this workbook to build a stronger relationship with God and your spouse. Take your time as you answer workbook questions and seek God for understanding in your life.

The Wife 101 workbook is a great tool for women's groups, book clubs, or individual study. I would love to hear from you about how this workbook is blessing you and your group. Correspondence can be emailed to me at drajwilson@gmail.com or via the contact form on www.andreawilsononline.com.

Happy Reading & Journaling!

A'ndrea J. Wilson, Ph.D.

Lesson 1: The Reason Why He Won't Marry You

Therefore a man shall leave his father and his mother and shall become united and cleave to his wife, and they shall become one flesh. (Genesis 2:24)

In Lesson 1, Amber learns that her ex-boyfriend Chris is marrying another woman. This is painful news for Amber because she has invested so much time and energy into a man who did not perceive her as "wife material." Chris ends the chapter stating that she was too independent and needed to let the man be the man in the relationship. How did you feel about Amber's lunch with Chris and his behavior?

_____

_____

_____

_____

_____

Is there such a thing as being "too independent" or women not letting men play their role as men? Have you ever been accused of this? Do you believe that men and woman have different roles to play?

_____

_____

_____

_____

Genesis 2:24 describes the nature of a couple coming together in marriage. Read this verse and write down your thoughts about what this verse means for men, women, and the married couple.

_____

_____

_____

_____

_____

_____

_____

_____

_____

_____

_____

_____

_____

_____

_____

_____

_____

_____

_____

_____

_____

_____

_____

_____

Lesson 2: Your Friends (Especially the Single Ones) Don't Know Anything!

There is a way that seems right to a man and appears straight before him, but at the end of it is the way of death.

(Proverbs 14:12)

In Lesson 2, Amber confides in her best friend, Tisha, who gives her some bad advice. Have you ever talked to one of your friends about a relationship problem? What kind of advice did they give you? How do you know what advice to take and what to dismiss?

_____

_____

_____

_____

_____

Tisha tells Amber that Chris is probably intimidated by her. Intimidated is another word to describe being afraid or scared. Do you believe that men in general are afraid or scared of women? Why or why not? Why do women suggest that men are intimidated by them?

_____

_____

_____

_____

_____

Amber, following the advice of Tisha, ends up on a date with an exotic dancer at Chris's engagement party. If you would have been in Amber's shoes, would you have gone along with Tisha's plan? Why or why not? How should Amber have dealt with the situation?

_____

_____

_____

_____

_____

Read Proverbs 14:12. Discuss your thoughts about what this verse means especially as if relates to marriage and relationships.

_____

_____

_____

_____

_____

_____

_____

_____

_____

_____

_____

_____

_____

Lesson 3: Align Yourself with Wise Women Who Can Edify You

He who deals wisely and heeds [God's] word and counsel shall find good, and whoever leans on, trusts in, and is confident in the Lord–happy, blessed, and fortunate is he. (Proverbs 16:20)

In Lesson 3, Amber attends church and signs up to take a course for women called "Wife 101." The goal of the class is to teach women how to be more effective in their relationships. Have you ever taken a course on relationships or participated in group counseling for a relationship issue? How does taking a class or group work help people grow and develop personally? Are there any courses or groups in your area that you can join or enroll in? If not, are you willing to create one?

_____

_____

_____

_____

_____

Amber wakes up feeling depressed about her life, but listens to inspirational music and attends church to help her overcome her negative emotions. How can depression and other negative emotions be dangerous if you allow yourself to wallow in these feelings? Outside of the two actions Amber takes, what things can you do when you are feeling down that will lift your spirits?

_____

_____

_____

_____

Read Proverbs 16:20. Write down your thoughts and feelings about this verse. Are there godly people in your life who can give you wise counsel? List the names of these people.

_____

_____

_____

_____

_____

_____

_____

_____

_____

_____

_____

_____

_____

_____

_____

_____

_____

_____

_____

_____

_____

_____

_____

_____

Lesson 4: Be Someone He Can Take Home to His Momma

The words of Lemuel, King of Massa, which his mother taught him: What, my son? What, son of my womb? What [shall I advise you], son of my vows and dedication to God? Give not your strength to [loose] women, nor your ways to those who and that which ruin and destroy kings. (Proverbs 31:1-3)

"For those of you who are mothers already, think about your children. If you have a son, think about him. If you don't have children or don't have a son, imagine that you had a son. Imagine that this son was at the age where he wanted to date and even get married. Now imagine that he was willing to sit down with you and allow you to give him advice concerning the type of woman that he should date and marry. What would you tell him? He is listening and willing to hear anything you want to tell him about women, dating, and marriage. Specifically, what traits would you tell him to look for in a wife? Now, let's up the ante. Not only is this your son, but you are the queen of your country, your husband has died, and your son is now the king of the land! Not only do you want your son to have a good wife because you want the best for your son, but who he chooses as a wife will be the next queen! She will impact both him and the nation. Now, what traits and qualities would you advise your son to look for in a wife?"

During the first Wife 101 class, Lydia asked her students to consider the qualities and traits they would want their sons to look for in a spouse. Use the lines below to write down the traits you would want the wife of your son to possess.

_____

_____

_____

_____

_____

_____

_____

_____

_____

Lydia closed her bible and looked out at us. "I want you all to take some time right now to write a list of all the things about yourself that makes you a good woman, wife, and mother. Even if you do not have children or are not married, write down the qualities that you possess that would make you a good wife or mother. Be as detailed as possible. I will give you fifteen minutes of quiet time to create your lists."

The women in the Wife 101 class were asked to write down their own qualities that they believed made them good women. Take fifteen minutes to create your own list. What characteristics do you possess that makes you a good woman, wife, and/or mother?

_____

_____

_____

_____

_____

_____

_____

_____

_____

_____

_____

_____

_____

_____

_____

_____

Lesson 5: You Don't Have to Have the Last Word

A continual dripping on a day of violent showers and a contentious woman are alike; Whoever attempts to restrain [a contentious woman] might as well try to stop the wind–his right hand encounters oil [and she slips through his fingers].

(Proverbs 27:15-16)

In Lesson 5, Amber finds herself competing during a meeting with a potential business partner. Have you ever felt that you were competing with a man in your career or in your personal relationships? Do you feel that Amber handled the situation the right way or was there another manner in which she should have addressed the problem?

_____

_____

_____

_____

_____

Samuel Perkins, another potential business partner, tells her that she doesn't always have to have the last word. Do you ever find yourself in situations where you are fighting to have the last word? If so, what does being the last person to speak mean to you? Has having the last word helped or hurt the relationship or situation?

_____

_____

_____

_____

Amber's employee Eric tells her that a man's role is as the head (leader), and suggests that it is difficult for a woman to be in leadership positions outside the home and then properly submit herself to her husband once she gets home. Do you agree or disagree that a man should be the leader? Should a man's headship be limited to the home or continue into other aspects of society? Do you ever find yourself struggling with transitioning from a position of authority to a position of submission?

_____

_____

_____

_____

_____

_____

_____

_____

Read Proverbs 27:15-16. Write down your thoughts about the meaning of these verses and how they apply to your life.

_____

_____

_____

_____

_____

_____

_____

_____

Lesson 6: Be a Jewel

A capable, intelligent, and virtuous woman – who is he who can find her? She is far more precious than jewels and her value is far above rubies or pearls. The heart of her husband trusts in her confidently and relies on and believes in her securely, so that he has no lack of [honest] gain or need of [dishonest] spoil. (Proverbs 31:10-11)

"Some of you may think that you are virtuous women already. I will not say that you aren't, but I am confident that by the time we go through these lessons and examine the many aspects of virtue, many of you who think you're virtuous will realize that you are not as virtuous as you thought you were."

During the second class, Lydia challenged the women to really consider if they are actually virtuous women. Read page 27 in your book. Do you believe that you are already a virtuous woman? Why or why not?

_____

_____

_____

_____

_____

Lydia asked the ladies to answer several questions on pages 28-29. Please write down your answers to the following questions:

Do you work a job outside of your home? _____

Do you work from home? _____

Do you consider yourself a housewife or at-home mother, not holding a paying job? _____

If you do work a job, do you feel you must work because of your family's financial obligations? _____

Do you believe that if you did not work, your husband could be the sole provider for the family? _____

Are you concerned that if times got hard or if your husband was tempted that he would involve himself in wicked or illegal activities to gain money or possessions? _____

Why do you think Lydia asked the ladies these questions? After answering the questions for yourself, what thoughts and emotions about your answers do you have?

_____

_____

_____

_____

_____

"If you want your husband to be a better man, you have to become a better woman. It is time to stop asking God to change him and time to start asking God to change you. This is why First Corinthians 7:14 states that the unbelieving husband is consecrated by his wife. As a married union, what we do as women is connected to what happens to our men. We have to stop playing the blame game, shooting our men down for their faults, and start asking ourselves, what do I need to do to become a better woman that will result in him becoming a better man?"

Read page 30. Write down your thoughts and feelings about Lydia's statements to the class.

_____

_____

_____

_____

_____

"For your homework, I want you to read and meditate on verses twelve and thirteen. I also want you to create a list. Write down all of the things that you have to do within a week to help keep your home and family in order. If you are not married, pretend that you are and list the things you would need to do if you had a husband. If you do not have children, pretend that you have at least one child and list all of the things you would need to do for a school aged child. This list should include household chores, childcare activities, and other wifely duties such as sex and communication with your husband. Do not include any activities that you do for your own career. Attached to each duty the average amount of time it takes you to do that activity each week. For example, it may take you six hours per week to wash everyone in your

family's clothes, iron, fold, and put them away. If you have more children it may take longer. But write down an estimated time for each activity."

Create a list of your own activities and time spent on the lines below.

_____

_____

_____

_____

_____

_____

_____

_____

_____

_____

_____

_____

_____

_____

_____

_____

_____

_____

_____

_____

_____

_____

_____

_____

_____

_____

_____

Lesson 7: Never Underestimate the Little Guy

But the Lord said to Samuel, Look not on his appearance or at the height of his stature, for I have rejected him. For the Lord sees not as man sees; for man looks on the outward appearance, but the Lord looks on the heart.

(I Samuel 16:7)

In Lesson 7, Amber finds herself in a jam when she is expected to show up at a business function with a date. Because of her competitive relationship with Jonathan Gold, she ends up lying then needs Eric to help her save face. Is there anyone in your life who has this effect on you? Why do we allow others who are not important to us to affect our emotions and behaviors?

_____

_____

_____

_____

_____

During their trip to Savannah, Amber and Eric get a chance to know each other more personally rather than professionally. Amber realizes that she has never taken the time to connect with Eric despite the fact that he has worked for her for years. Are there people in your life (male and female) that you associate with, but have never taken the time to get to know who they are? Could these relationships become friendships? What is holding you back from getting to know these people on a personal level?

_____

_____

_____

Read I Samuel 16:7. Write down your thoughts and feelings about the meaning of this verse and how it applies to your own life.

_____

_____

_____

_____

_____

_____

_____

_____

_____

_____

_____

_____

_____

_____

_____

_____

_____

_____

_____

_____

_____

_____

_____

_____

_____

Lesson 8: Maintain a Drama-Free Zone

She comforts, encourages, and does him only good as long as there is life within her. She seeks out wool and flax and works with willing hands [to develop it]. (Proverbs 31:12-13)

During the Wife 101 class, Lydia had the ladies add up the amount of time on their activity lists. Please read pages 41-43 in your Wife 101 book. Also return to your created activity list in Lesson 6 of this workbook and add up your total hours. Add up your activities hours without considering the amount of time you spend working a paying job. Add up the number of hours you spend on your job plus travel time. Add the two previous numbers together. Write these numbers on the appropriate lines below.

A: Total hours from activity list: _____

B: Total working hours: _____

C: Total hours from activity list plus working hours (A+B): _____

D: Subtract 112 from your total on line C: _____

Lydia calculated several numbers for her class. Here are those numbers for your convenience:

Total hours available in a week: 168

Average hours of sleep in a week: 56

Total full-time working hours in a week: 45

Hours available in a week minus average sleep time: 112

Hours available in a week minus average sleep time and work time: 67

Average number of hours per day remaining for a woman with a full-time job: 9.5

Average number of hours per day remaining for a woman without a full-time job: 16

Your total on Line D represents the amount of hours you have remaining after you do everything you need to do within a week. Your number may be a negative number which means that you are probably either not getting enough sleep or are cutting corners in your family, personal, or work life. Write down your thoughts and feelings about this activity and your results. Are there any changes that you need to make based on your results?

_____

_____

_____

_____

_____

_____

_____

_____

_____

"But this virtuous woman is a drama free woman. When that man comes home in a foul mood, complaining about his job, she says, 'Baby it's gonna be okay. God is with you.' When he gets laid off and can't find work for six months she says, 'God will provide, just keep the faith.' When she finds out that he has gambled their bill money away, does she curse him out and leave with the kids? No. She tells him, 'I'm praying for you, that God will help you make good decisions that will help our family and not hurt it.' How many of you could do that all the time?"

Read page 44 and Proverbs 31:12. Why is it so difficult to *always* comfort, encourage, and treat your mate with goodness?

_____

_____

_____

_____

_____

Read pages 45-46. What was the point that Lydia was trying to make to her students about work? How do you feel about your job or working? How does your work life impact your faith?

_____

_____

_____

_____

_____

_____

_____

_____

_____

_____

_____

_____

_____

_____

_____

_____

_____

_____

_____

_____

_____

_____

_____

_____

_____

_____

Lesson 9: Appreciate the Little Things

Better is little with the reverent, worshipful fear of the Lord than great and rich treasure and trouble with it.

(Proverbs 15:16)

In Lesson 9, Amber tries to avoid Valentine's Day. Many single and married people struggle with the holidays because it reminds them of the things they that do not have. Is there a holiday or occasion that you try to avoid? What are your fears connected to this day or event? What can you do to cope and overcome your reservations about this day?

_____

_____

_____

_____

_____

Eric makes a statement to Amber about how her accomplishments may impact a man's feeling of worth. Read page 48-49 and write down your thoughts about Amber and Eric's conversation.

_____

_____

_____

_____

_____

At the end of the chapter, Eric opens up to Amber about his feelings, causing Amber to feel fear and reflect on the pain of her past. How does past hurt that we hold on to keep us from moving forward? Is there any pain from your past that keeps you fearful of something new? Write it down.

_____

_____

_____

_____

_____

Read Proverbs 15:16. Write down your thoughts and feelings about this verse.

_____

_____

_____

_____

_____

_____

_____

_____

_____

_____

_____

_____

_____

_____

Lesson 10: Work the Night Shift

She is like the merchant ships loaded with foodstuffs; she brings her household's food from a far [country]. She rises while it is yet night and gets [spiritual] food for her household and assigns her maids their tasks. (Proverbs 31:14-15)

"What are you bringing to the table? Is it a bunch of typical possessions: a house, car, bank account, etc? Or do you have more to offer? See, eventually the money will run out, the house can fall apart, or the car might breakdown, but traits like wisdom, kindness, honesty, gentleness, understanding, faith, passion, compassion, and authenticity never get lost in the shuffle. You can always pull from them for nourishment."

Read pages 55-56 of the Wife 101 book. What are you bringing to the table?

_____

_____

_____

_____

_____

Lydia smiled then glanced downwards and pulled her bible closer to her face. "Verse fifteen reads, 'She rises while it is yet night and gets spiritual food for her household and assigns her maids their tasks.' If any of you are regularly waking up after the sun rises, I'm about to rain on your parade. You are going to have to start waking up earlier. Why? Because the devil and his angels don't sleep in! Don't believe me? Turn on the morning news. While you were getting your beauty rest, the enemy was working overtime. Somebody got shot, someone else was robbed, two people were murdered, there was a car accident with injuries, suicides, drugs, gangs, weapons in schools, homosexuality, rapes, child molestations, teen pregnancies, AIDS, and adultery; do I have to go on? Your family has to go out into a world filled with a myriad of evils, and you are letting them go unprotected because you are in the bed asleep.

Read pages 57-58. What are you doing to prepare your family for their day? What time do you get up? Do you pray for your family before they start their day? Write down your thoughts about Proverbs 31:15 and how it influences the type of wife you are or want to be. What changes do you plan to make so that you can work the night shift?

_____

_____

_____

_____

_____

_____

_____

_____

_____

_____

_____

_____

_____

_____

_____

_____

_____

_____

_____

_____

_____

_____

Lesson 11: Stand For Something or Fall For Anything

The foolish woman is noisy; she is simple and open to all forms of evil, she [willfully and recklessly] knows nothing whatever [of eternal value]. (Proverbs 9:13)

In Lesson 11, Amber finds out she has an unexpected admirer. Although she not interested in her admirer, she agrees to go out on a date with him. Why do you think she agrees to the date? Do you think she is desperate? Why do we sometimes go along with things that are not in our hearts to do?

_____

_____

_____

_____

_____

On page 64-65 Amber is compared to a man she despises. Have you ever been told something about yourself that was meant as a compliment, but made you feel awful? What did these words mean to Amber? What did those words mean for you?

_____

_____

_____

_____

_____

While Amber is on a date, she runs into her ex-boyfriend. Why does it seem that people are more attracted to others who are with someone else or already taken? How would you have handled Chris if you were Amber?

_____

_____

_____

_____

_____

Read Proverbs 9:13. Write down your thoughts and feelings about this verse.

_____

_____

_____

_____

_____

_____

_____

_____

_____

_____

_____

_____

_____

_____

_____

_____

_____

Lesson 12: Know When to Say No

She considers a [new] field before she buys or accepts it [expanding prudently and not courting neglect of her present duties by assuming other duties]; with her savings [of time and strength] she plants fruitful vines in her vineyard. She girds herself with strength [spiritual, mental, and physical fitness for her God-given task] and makes her arms strong and firm. (Proverbs 31:16-17)

Lydia continued, "I call this the Superwoman Syndrome. So many of us are walking around here with the letter S on our chests. Although you think you can do everything, the enemy is wreaking havoc around you because you've left holes. Your family is neglected, your friends are neglected, you are neglected, your husband is neglected, and most importantly, your God is neglected. You are so busy trying to impress this and that committee or group, who in the scope of things are unimportant, that the ones who really matter don't have access to you. Then you find yourself perplexed when your husband leaves you for another woman, your kids end up hanging with the wrong crowd, your friends don't answer your calls anymore, and your own health is deteriorating.

Read pages 70-73. Write down your thoughts and feelings about Proverbs 31:16 and Lydia's breakdown of what the verse means. Do you struggle with saying no? How can you overcome the need to people-please?

_____

_____

_____

_____

_____

_____

_____

_____

_____
_____
_____
_____
_____
_____
_____

Read Proverbs 31:17 and page 74. Write down your thoughts and feelings about this verse.

_____
_____
_____
_____
_____
_____
_____
_____
_____
_____
_____
_____
_____
_____
_____
_____
_____
_____

Lesson 13: Make a Bed You Are Willing to Lie In

Every wise woman builds her house, but the foolish one tears it down with her own hands. (Proverbs 14:1)

In Lesson 13, Amber is once again influenced by the advice of her best friend. Why do you think she keeps taking the advice of Tisha when it often leads her in a direction that she does not want to move in? Is there anyone in your life that steers you down the wrong path? Who are they and how can you avoid being negatively influenced by them?

_____

_____

_____

_____

_____

_____

_____

_____

_____

_____

In Amber's conversation with Eric, she begins to reveal to him information about her upbringing. Does this new information help you to understand Amber and her decisions? What people and situations from your upbringing shape the decisions you now make?

_____

_____

_____

_____

_____

_____

_____

_____

_____

Amber considers giving Chris another chance to date her despite how he has treated her in the past. Do you think it is wise for Amber to date Chris again? Why do we allow people from our past who have hurt us back into our lives again? Who have you allowed back into your life? Was it a good decision?

_____

_____

_____

_____

_____

_____

_____

_____

Read Proverbs 14:1. Write down your thoughts and feelings about this verse and how it applies to your life.

_____

_____

_____

_____

Lesson 14: Always Be a Star

She tastes and sees that her gain from work [with and for God] is good; her lamp goes not out, but burns on continually through the night [of trouble, privation, or sorrow, warning away fear, doubt, and distrust]. She lays her hands to the spindle, and her hands hold the distaff. (Proverbs 31:18-19)

"The first part of verse eighteen says that her experience has shown her that working with and for God, doing the right thing, trusting Him, and living for Him has resulted in good gain, positive results, desirable outcomes. Because of her experience she knows that she doesn't have to flip out every time something stressful comes her way. Her lamp continually burns on. When the bills are due she says, 'God, I trust you.' When they tell her that her child might be ADD or autistic she says, 'God, I know your plan is perfect.' When her husband dies she says, 'God, I know you are with me.' Her lamp burns on. There is no temporary outage of electricity or shortage of oil. Her experience has taught her that God is still in control and that there is no need to become upset or be afraid. Just keep shining and be like a bright star in the midst of a dark night."

Read Proverbs 31:18-19, as well as pages 87 through 90 in your Wife 101 book. Write down your thoughts and feelings about these verses and how they impact your life. Especially consider the following questions: How do you react to negative circumstances? Are you able to keep your light shining constantly or does it go out in the midst of trouble? Do you require that things always go your way or constantly have the need to be in control? Are you skillful? Do you take the time to complete tasks in the spirit of excellence?

_____

_____

_____

_____

_____

_____

Lesson 15: Listen More Than You Speak

A [self-confident] fool's lips bring contention, and his mouth invites a beating. A [self-confident] fool's mouth is his ruin, and his lips are a snare to himself. (Proverbs 18:6-7)

In Lesson 15, Amber decides to listen during a business meeting instead of speaking and gains new insight about the people she is meeting with. Read pages 91-93. What do you think about what happens when she stops "power struggling" with Gold? Do you speak more than you listen? What might happen if you listened more than you spoke?

_____

_____

_____

_____

_____

_____

_____

_____

_____

Read Proverbs 18:6-7. Write down your thoughts about these verses and how they apply to you.

_____

_____

_____

Lesson 16: Cover Up!

She opens her hand to the poor, yes, she reaches out her filled hands to the needy [whether in body, mind, or spirit]. She fears not the snow for her family, for all her household are doubly clothed in scarlet. (Proverbs 31:20-21)

"Verse twenty doesn't say she gives to the poor once a year when she cleans out her closet or on Christmas. It doesn't say she gives a few dollars to her church and hopes they will handle feeding the poor in her neighborhood. It says that she opens and reaches out her filled hands to the poor and needy. She is the one organizing the clothing drive. She is the one going down to the soup kitchen once a month or even once a week. She is inviting people into her home, feeding them, and sending them away with a plate. She is scraping up some money to help pay a light bill or water bill...and wait! She gives than says, 'Don't worry about paying me back.' She drives that mother down from the street to the welfare office or to a charity to get help to find shoes for those six kids. Giving is not a one-time thing. Giving is not complacent. Giving is not passive. Giving is active, aggressive, ongoing, and intentional."

Read Proverbs 31:20 and pages 97-99 of the Wife 101 book. What kind of giver are you? Are there ways in which you could be giving that you are not? Discuss your thoughts about this verse and Lydia's lecture on it.

_____

_____

_____

_____

_____

_____

_____

_____

_____

_____

"Ladies, we have to start covering up. We have to prepare our families for the rainy days by covering them spiritually, mentally, and physically. If I send my child outside in January without a coat or jacket, the Department of Family and Children Services is going to come to my house and tell me that I am neglecting my child because I haven't prepared him for the harsh weather. That child needs to be covered and protected from the cold. In the same manner, we have to cover our entire family, dipping them twice in the blood of Jesus."

Read Proverbs 31:21 and pages 99-100 in your Wife 101 book. Write down your thoughts about this verse and Lydia's explanation of it. Did you learn anything new? How can a woman prepare and protect her family?

_____

_____

_____

_____

_____

_____

_____

_____

_____

_____

_____

_____

_____

_____

_____

_____

_____

_____

_____

Lesson 17: Count the Costs

But he who did not know and did things worthy of a beating shall be beaten with few [lashes]. For everyone to whom much is given, of him shall much be required; and of him to whom men entrust much, they will require and demand all the more. (Luke 12:48)

In Lesson 17, Amber slows down her schedule for a week and takes time to reflect on how she is using what God has given to her. During that time, new and fresh ideas come to her about how she can help others. Do you ever take time out to review your life and how you are living it? What happens when we slow down and give God the opportunity to give us divine revelation?

_____

_____

_____

_____

_____

Tisha continues to disapprove of Amber's decisions in dating. Do you have friends who push you to do things their way even if you are uncomfortable with what they want you to do? If you were in Amber's shoes, how would you deal with someone like Tisha?

_____

_____

_____

_____

_____

The chapter ends with Amber agreeing to allow her mother and stepfather to temporarily live with her. Do you think this is a wise decision? Have you ever offered housing to a family member or friend in need? What happened? How can offering housing be beneficial? How can it be problematic?

_____

_____

_____

_____

_____

_____

_____

_____

_____

Read Luke 12:48. Write down your thoughts and feelings about this verse and how it applies to you.

_____

_____

_____

_____

_____

_____

_____

_____

_____

Lesson 18: Behind Every Great Man is a Virtuous Woman

She makes for herself coverlets, cushions, and rugs of tapestry. Her clothing is of linen, pure and fine, and of purple [such as that of which the clothing of the priest and the hallowed clothes of the temple were made]. Her husband is known in the [city's] gates, when he sits among the elders of the land. (Proverbs 31:22-23)

"Ladies, in the process of loving others and giving of yourselves, remember to love yourselves too. You deserve a 'me' day from time to time. It's okay to buy a new dress, get a pedicure, and splurge a little on a pair of those shoes you've been eyeing. The problem is not taking care of yourself or doing something nice for yourself. No, it occurs when your focus shifts to you, 24-7. It's when you think about nothing but you. It's when you're buying up the mall at the expense of bills that need to be paid. It's when you have to work two and three jobs to afford to shoe shop every week. Love yourself enough to treat yourself like royalty; however, love God enough to live with the mentality that it's not all about you, but about Him."

Read Proverbs 31:22 and pages 109-110. Write down your thoughts and feelings about this verse and Lydia's explanation of it. What is the difference between self-love/self-care and self-centeredness? How can you take care of yourself in the midst of caring for others?

_____

_____

_____

_____

_____

_____

_____

_____

_____

"He is known when he sits among the elders. He is known because of her. She is such an amazing woman that her virtue catapults him into celebrity status. Most great men are who they are because of the great women in their lives. Their success in the world is directly linked to our success as wives and mothers. For this reason, most elevated positions such as pastors, bishops, presidents, and other leaders, in order to be elected or appointed men are often required to be married. A good wife does more than just looks good on a man's arm; she thrusts him into his purpose. When you see a man who is living beneath his potential, often you also see a woman who is not exuding virtue."

Read Proverbs 31:23 and read page 111. Write down your thoughts and feelings about this verse and Lydia's insight. How is a man's status reflective of the woman in his life? How can you help your man to be a better leader?

_____

_____

_____

_____

_____

_____

_____

_____

_____

_____

_____

_____

_____

_____

Lesson 19: There's No Place Like Home

Seek, inquire for, and require the Lord while He may be found [claiming Him by necessity and by right]; call upon Him while he is near. Let the wicked forsake his way and the unrighteous man his thoughts; and let him return to the Lord, and He will have love, pity, and mercy for him, and to our God, for He will multiply to him His abundant pardon. For My thoughts are not your thoughts, neither are your ways My ways, says the Lord. (Isaiah 55:6-8)

In Lesson 19, Amber struggles with her relationship with her mother and stepfather. Do you have any negative emotions toward your parents or parental figures? How do these feelings interfere with your ability to get along with them? How is Amber's relationship with her parents a stronghold for her? How is your relationship with family members a stronghold for you?

_____

_____

_____

_____

_____

_____

_____

_____

_____

_____

_____

_____

_____

Amber has difficulty controlling her anger. Although she may have a reason to be upset, she often lashes out at the people in her life that she loves then feels guilty afterwards. Can you relate to Amber's dilemma? How should you respond to frustrating situations? How can you have better control over your anger?

_____

_____

_____

_____

_____

_____

_____

_____

_____

_____

Amber gets the opportunity to meet Eric's family. How important is it to meet someone's family and get along with them if you are considering dating them or marrying them? How does a person's family reflect the individual?

_____

_____

_____

_____

_____

_____

_____

_____

_____

Read Isaiah 55:6-8. Write down your thoughts and feelings about these verses and how they apply to your life.

_____

_____

_____

_____

_____

_____

_____

_____

_____

_____

_____

_____

_____

_____

_____

_____

_____

_____

_____

_____

_____

_____

Lesson 20: Be Prepared

She makes fine linen garments and leads others to buy them; she delivers to the merchants girdles [or sashes that free one up for service]. Strength and dignity are her clothing and her position is strong and secure; she rejoices over the future [the latter day or time to come, knowing that she and her family are in readiness for it]! (Proverbs 31:24-25)

"Although she has this business and opportunity to make money, she doesn't spend all of her time focusing on them. Her life is so much more than making money. Her life is balanced; selling things and monetary gain are only two small aspects of what makes her a wonderful woman, wife, and mother. She does not define herself by her business or money, and neither do others."

Read Proverbs 31:24. Based on the verse and the reading of Lesson 20, how is virtue demonstrated in the work/career life of a virtuous woman? What have you learned about working or making money from this chapter?

_____

_____

_____

_____

_____

_____

_____

_____

_____

_____

"Now I know that in our society we get consumed with name brand clothing. We feel good about ourselves when we are wearing clothing from stores like Anne Taylor, The Limited, Nordstrom's, Bloomingdale's, or Macy's. There is nothing wrong with shopping at these stores or wearing nice clothes, but contrary to popular belief, clothes don't make the woman. What is on the inside will always be revealed on the outside. I don't care how much you dress yourself up, if who you are ugly or weak on the inside, you inner character will override anything you are physically wearing."

Read Proverbs 31:25 and pages 134-136. How is a woman's character connected to her ability to handle whatever circumstances may arise? Do you put more energy into your physical clothing or your spiritual and mental clothing? Write down any thoughts or feelings you have about this verse.

_____

_____

_____

_____

_____

_____

_____

_____

_____

_____

_____

_____

_____

_____

_____

_____

_____

_____

_____

Lydia makes a few attempts to connect with Amber, but Amber is afraid of being transparent. Why is it important to have godly people in our lives with whom we can be honest with? Do you try to take on everything by yourself? How can you open up and allow God to use others to help you?

_____

_____

_____

_____

_____

_____

_____

_____

_____

_____

_____

_____

_____

_____

_____

_____

_____

_____

_____

_____

_____

Lesson 21: The Truth Shall Set You Free

And you will know the Truth, and the Truth will set you free. (John 8:32)

In Lesson 21, Amber learns that the business venture she is considering is not a good decision. Have you ever being planning to do something, but found out that it was risky? How did you respond? What is at stake if Amber foregoes her intuition and takes the risk anyway?

_____

_____

_____

_____

_____

_____

_____

_____

_____

_____

The truth comes out about Chris and Noel, helping Amber to make a choice about continuing to date Chris. Do you think she made the right decision? What factors did she use to make her decision? What factors do you use to make choices in your relationships?

_____

_____

_____

_____

_____

_____

_____

_____

_____

_____

Read John 8:32. Write down any thoughts or feelings you have about this verse and how it applies to you.

_____

_____

_____

_____

_____

_____

_____

_____

_____

_____

_____

_____

_____

_____

_____

_____

_____

_____

Lesson 22: If You Don't Have Something Nice To Say...

She opens her mouth in skillful and godly Wisdom, and on her tongue is the law of kindness [giving counsel and instruction]. She looks well to how things go in her household, and the bread of idleness (gossip, discontent, and self-pity) she will not eat. (Proverbs 31:26-27)

"As the woman of the house, you set the tone for the household. Your behavior and words will either positively or negatively influence the members of your family. If you are hostile, argumentative, gossipy, discontent, and whatnot, your family will often follow along and replicate that attitude. However, if you are peaceful, joyful, faithful, appreciative, optimistic, kind, and loving, your family will often follow suit. Peace in your home begins and ends with you. If your home is constantly in chaos, before you blame your angry husband or wayward child, first take a look at yourself and assess whether or not you have unintentionally set a negative tone in your household."

Read Proverbs 31:26-27 and pages 146-147 in the Wife 101 book. Write down your thoughts and feelings about these verses and Lydia's explanation of them. Are you guilty of eating the bread of idleness? What are the consequences of allowing negativity into your home through your thoughts, words, and actions?

_____

_____

_____

_____

_____

_____

_____

_____

_____

_____

Lesson 23: Choose Wisely

And if it seems evil to you to serve the Lord, Chose for yourselves this day whom you will serve, whether the gods which your fathers served on the other side of the River, or the gods of the Amorites, in whose land you dwell; but for me and my house, we will serve the Lord. (Joshua 24:15)

In Lesson 23, Amber receives a proposal. How do you feel about her answer to the proposal and how she deals with the people in her life following her response?

_____

_____

_____

_____

_____

Read pages 154-156. Amber's mother and stepfather attempt to provide her with wisdom concerning marriage. What are your thoughts about their guidance?

_____

_____

_____

_____

_____

Read Joshua 24:25. Write down your thoughts and feelings about this verse and how it applies to your life.

_____

_____

_____

_____

_____

_____

_____

_____

_____

_____

_____

_____

_____

_____

_____

_____

_____

_____

_____

_____

_____

_____

_____

_____

_____

Lesson 24: Make Them Proud

Her children rise up and call her blessed (happy, fortunate, and to be envied); and her husband boasts of and praises her, [saying], Many daughters have done virtuously, nobly, and well [with the strength of character that is steadfast in goodness], but you excel them all. (Proverbs 31:28-29)

"Here's the interesting part. Her husband doesn't say that his wife is fine or hot. He doesn't say she's a good cook or keeps the house clean. He doesn't mention that she still has a Coke bottle shape or flawless skin. No. He says, 'There are a lot of great women out here, but my wife is better than all of them!' Wow! Now that is a compliment. When you have got a husband saying things like that about you, you never have to worry about him cheating or not coming home at night. Insecurity flies out the door because this man just said that no other woman compares to you."

In Lesson 24, Lydia talks to her students about the perception that the virtuous woman's children and husband have of her. Read this lesson and write down what you believe that your children and husband think of you based on their words and behaviors. If you are single and/or childless, how do other men or people around you perceive you? How do you feel about others' perceptions of you? If you are not comfortable with their perception of you, what can you do to change this?

_____

_____

_____

_____

_____

_____

_____

_____

Lesson 25: Handle Your Affairs Before They Handle You

[Put first things first.] Prepare your work outside and get it ready for yourself in the field; and afterward build your house and establish your home. (Proverbs 24:27)

In Lesson 25, the inevitable happens: Amber's secret is exposed. Why do we keep secrets that we know will eventually come out? Why do you think Amber procrastinates being honest with the men in her life?

_____

_____

_____

_____

_____

Is there something in your life that you need to handle, but are avoiding? Why? Write down your plan to deal with your situation before it spirals out of control.

_____

_____

_____

_____

_____

_____

_____

_____

_____

Read Proverbs 24:27. Write down your thoughts and feelings about this verse and how it relates to your life.

_____

_____

_____

_____

_____

_____

_____

_____

_____

_____

_____

_____

_____

_____

_____

_____

_____

_____

_____

_____

_____

_____

_____

_____

_____

_____

Lesson 26: Produce What Lasts

Charm and grace are deceptive, and beauty is vain [because it is not lasting], but a woman who reverently and worshipfully fears the Lord, she shall be praised! Give her the fruit of her hands, and let her own works praise her in the gates [of the city]! (Proverbs 31:30-31)

Charm and grace are deceptive. Turn to page 165 in your Wife 101 book and read it. Write down your thoughts about the discussion on charm and grace.

_____

_____

_____

_____

_____

Beauty is vain. Read pages 165-166. Write down your thoughts about the discussion on beauty.

_____

_____

_____

_____

_____

Amber mental debates her self-reliance and inability to maintain her focus on God on page 166. Do you struggle with the same issues? If so, what is the first step to beginning to trust and depend on God?

_____

_____

_____

_____

_____

The last question on page 166 is "What does my life say about me?" Ask yourself this question and write down your answers, thoughts, or feelings.

_____

_____

_____

_____

_____

_____

_____

_____

_____

_____

_____

_____

_____

_____

_____

_____

_____

_____

Lesson 27: Forgive and Let Go

For if you forgive people of their trespasses [their reckless and willful sins, leaving them, letting them go, and giving up resentment], your heavenly Father will also forgive you. (Matthew 6:14)

In Lesson 27, a crisis reveals the truth about the people in Amber's life, as well as her need to forgive and let go. Read the entire chapter and write down your thoughts and feelings about the power of forgiveness? Who in your life do you need to forgive? What do you need to let go of? Ask God to help you forgive and let go.

_____

_____

_____

_____

_____

_____

_____

_____

_____

_____

_____

_____

_____

_____

_____

_____

_____

_____

Read Matthew 6:14. What does this verse mean for you? Why is it so important to forgive others?

_____

_____

_____

_____

_____

_____

_____

_____

_____

_____

_____

_____

_____

_____

_____

_____

_____

_____

_____

_____

_____

_____

_____

_____

_____

_____

Lesson 28: Know A Few Good Recipes

Through skillful and godly Wisdom is a house (a life, a home, a family) built, and by understanding it is established [on a sound and good foundation], And by knowledge shall its chambers [of every area] be filled with all precious and pleasant riches. (Proverbs 24:3-4)

During the last Wife 101 class, Lydia returned the "qualities list" back to her students and asked them to compare their lists to the traits of a virtuous woman. Turn back in your workbook to Lesson 4 and compare and contrast your list to the list below. Put a check mark next to the qualities you already had on your original list. Put an X next to the qualities that you did not indicate that you had in your original list, but feel that you currently possess. Put a star next to the qualities that you feel that you do not have and need to develop in.

1. Rare
2. Valuable
3. Capable
4. Intelligent
5. Honorable
6. Trustworthy
7. Motivating
8. Comforting
9. Encouraging
10. Merciful
11. Willing
12. Resourceful
13. Hard-working
14. Preparer

15. Prayer Warrior

16. Does Not Over-obligate

17. Prioritizes

18. Conserver

19. Mentally Strong

20. Physically Strong

21. Spiritually Strong

22. Faithful

23. Illuminating

24. Skillful

25. Giving

26. Loving

27. Protects

28. Covers

29. Practices Self-care

30. Positively Influences Her Husband's Success

31. Persuasive

32. A Businesswoman

33. Dignified

34. Wise

35. Kind

36. Content

37. A Blessing to Her Family

38. Authentic

39. God-fearing

40. Fruitful

Review your list and tally your check marks, X's, and stars.

Number of Check Marks: _____

Number of X's: _____

Number of Stars: _____

How do you feel about the qualities you do and do not possess? Are you encouraged or discouraged about your list? Are you willing to work on the areas that are undeveloped? What can you do to become more like the virtuous woman?

_____

_____

_____

_____

_____

Lydia spoke with Amber after the final class about her situations at home, work, and in her love life. She had been praying about her life, but felt as if God was ignoring her. What she did not see was that God was working on her behalf the entire time and using others like Lydia to support her. Have you ever felt like Amber, that God was not moving or answering your prayers? Think back to a time when something you prayed about worked out in your favor in the end despite not getting an immediate answer. Write down that experience and what you learned from it about God's timing and sovereignty.

_____

_____

_____

_____

_____

Lydia reached over and patted my hand which rested on the arm of the chair. "Life with God is not a life that can be controlled by us. It is filled with the what ifs. The one thing that we can rest in is that God knows what is best for us. When we trust Him and submit to His will, we allow Him to gives us the best, what He always had in mind for us. God loves you, and He knows your heart. I know that it is difficult to walk away from something you've always wanted, but if God tells you to wait, trust Him and He will give you more than you ever imagined was possible. Faith is the substance of things hoped for, the evidence of things not seen."

Amber struggles with her decision to choose between Gold, Chris, and Eric throughout the process of her taking the Wife 101 course. A lot of her hesitation to choose is due to her fears. This fear causes her to act desperately at times, as well as to try to control things that are beyond her control. How often do you let fear grip you in this manner? Are you currently trying to control things that should be placed in God's hands? Can any of your behaviors or thoughts be considered desperate? How can you move away from fear and towards faith?

_____

_____

_____

_____

_____

_____

_____

_____

_____

_____

_____

_____

_____

_____

_____

_____

_____

Lesson 29: All That Glitters Isn't Gold

My fruit is better than gold, yes, than refined gold, and my increase than choice silver. I [Wisdom] walk in the way of righteousness (moral and spiritual rectitude in every area and relation), in the midst of the paths of justice, That I may cause those who love me to inherit [true] riches and that I may fill their treasuries. (Proverbs 8:19-21)

In Lesson 29, Amber is forced to make both a business decision and a heart decision. Read pages 186-190. Do you think that Amber made the right decision in both cases? Why or why not? Are there decisions in your life that need to be made? If so, what are they and what do you believe is the right thing to do?

_____

_____

_____

_____

_____

_____

_____

_____

_____

_____

_____

_____

_____

_____

Read Proverbs 8:19-21. Write down your thoughts and feelings about these verses.

_____

_____

_____

_____

_____

_____

_____

_____

_____

_____

_____

_____

_____

_____

_____

_____

_____

_____

_____

_____

_____

_____

_____

_____

_____

_____

Lesson 30: He Knows Your Name Because It's His Own

Then Adam said, This [creature] is now bone of my bones and flesh of my flesh; she shall be called Woman, because she was taken out of man. (Genesis 2:23)

Amber and her mother have a heart-to-heart conversation in Lesson 30. Amber struggles to say what she wants because she feels the situation is hopeless. Her mother encourages her to not only speak what she wants, but to also pray about the matter and put her hope in God. Is there some issue in your life that you feel hopeless about? Write it down and then pray to God about that issue.

_____

_____

_____

_____

_____

As Amber is driving, the Voice of God speaks to her and gives her instructions. Do you believe that you can hear from God? How does God speak to you? Do you recognize God's voice when He is speaking? How important is it to obey the Voice of God?

_____

_____

_____

_____

_____

Read pages 198-199. Amber does something really unexpected at her wedding. How do you feel about what she gave her husband? Could you give your husband something so valuable? What was her point of giving this gift? How do you feel about the manner in which she gave it to him, and what does this say about what potentially waits down the road for them as a married couple?

_____

_____

_____

_____

_____

_____

_____

_____

_____

_____

Read Genesis 2:23. Write down your thoughts and feelings about this verse and its meaning.

_____

_____

_____

_____

_____

_____

_____

_____

_____

_____

Epilogue
Lesson 31: To Everything There Is a Time

He has made everything beautiful in its time. (Ecclesiastes 3:11)

Read Ecclesiastes 3:1-11. Write down your thoughts and feelings about these verses. What is God speaking to you about right now, telling you that His timing is perfect?

_____

_____

_____

_____

_____

_____

_____

_____

_____

_____

_____

_____

_____

_____

_____

_____

_____

_____

_____

_____

_____

_____

_____

_____

_____

_____

_____

_____

_____

_____

_____

_____

_____

_____

_____

_____

_____

_____

_____

_____

_____

_____

_____

_____

_____

_____

_____

Notes

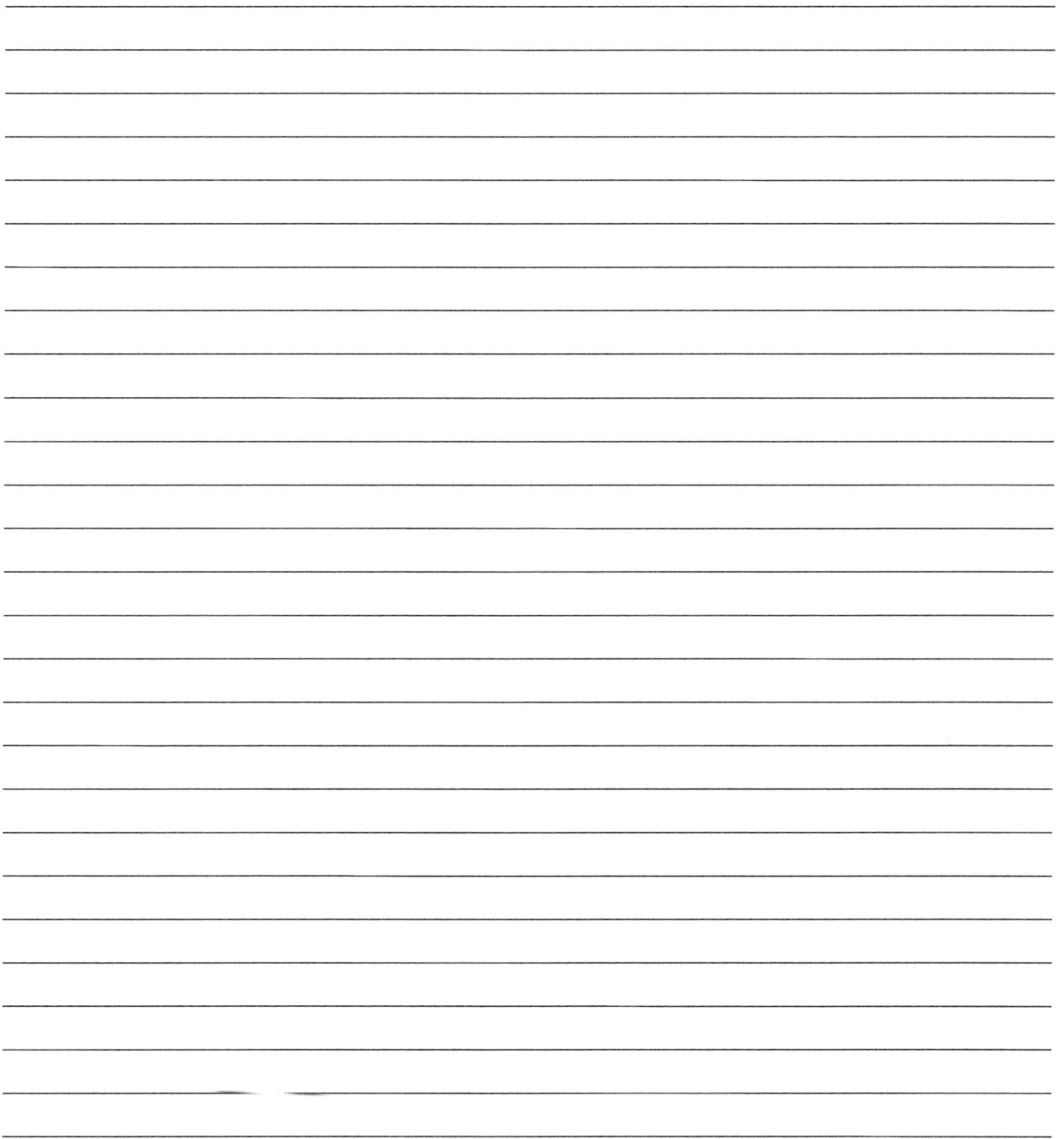

Acknowledgements

God: You amaze me every day. Thank You for this gift and for making a way when there is no way. Wise men still seek You and so do I.

Mom & Dad: My lifelong supporters. Thank you for always being a phone call away when I need you most.

Family & Friends: Thanks to all of my family and friends who have supported me in one way or another. Special thanks to Team A'ndrea (LOL): Kesha, Tanisha, Sharitta, Chemeka, Mary Jane, and Antonio.

Chi Pi Zeta Chapter of Zeta Phi Beta Sorority, Inc.: Thanks to my sisters for your continued support of my writing career and me as an individual: Debra, Connie, LaRita, Alisha, Sonja, Sandra, Yvette, E-Beth, Denise, Lucinda, Rhonda C., Rhonda L., Iris, Regina, Liletha, Korri, Catreva, Temirra, Aleesha, and all of our new and future members.

Authors: Special thanks to Norlita Brown, Yolanda King Stephen, Michelle Stimpson, Kendra Norman-Bellamy & M-PACT, Vanessa Richardson, TaNisha Webb, Christian Authors on Tour, and every author who has positively impacted my writing career.

Book Clubs: For those who have already read Wife 101 and for those who will read it, I thank you for your support, and I hope the novel and workbook stir thoughtful discussions. Special thanks to OOSA Online Book Club, Candler County Book Club (G.A.), Exquisite Ladies Book Club (N.J.), and the Treutlen County Library Book Club (G.A.) who were amongst the first book clubs to read Wife 101 and inspire The Wife 101 Workbook.

Readers: This workbook was especially designed for you. I never wanted to create it, but your feedback pushed me through my reservations. I pray that this tool helps you to take the next step towards being the best woman, mother, and wife you can be – a virtuous woman.

Remember, I love you, but most importantly, God loves you!

Andrea

About the Author

A'ndrea J. Wilson, Ph.D. is the author of both fiction and nonfiction books, including the novel, *Wife 101*, and the devotional, *My Business His Way: Wisdom & Inspiration for Entrepreneurs*. She holds a Bachelor's of Science in Psychology, a Master's of Science in Counseling Psychology; Marriage and Family Therapy, and a Doctorate in Global Leadership; Educational Leadership. A'ndrea works as a college professor, as well as conducts workshops on a variety of personal and professional topics. Dr. Wilson is the Founder and President of Divine Garden Press, a publishing company that specializes in fiction and nonfiction books addressing marriage and family issues. She is a member of Zeta Phi Beta Sorority, Inc. and is frequently involved in community service activities. A native of Rochester, New York, she currently resides in Georgia. Please visit her online at www.andreawilsononline.com or email her at drajwilson@gmail.com.

Other Books by A'ndrea J. Wilson

Nonfiction

My Business His Way: Wisdom & Inspiration for Entrepreneurs

Kiss & Tell: Releasing Expectations

The Wife 101 Workbook

Fiction

Wife 101

Husband 101 (November 2012)

The Things We Said We Would Never Do

Ready & Able Teens: Ebony's Bad Habit

Ready & ABLE Teens: Desiree Dishes the Dirt

Ready & ABLE Teens: Victor Rocks the Vote (November 2012)